ECHOES OF THE SOUL

STORIES THAT SING, WORDS THAT WEAVE

KANNAL THAMIZH S

To the dreamers who chase the wind,
to the wanderers who listen to silence,
to the ones who see poetry in the smallest moments—
this book is for you.

For those who find beauty in both light and shadow,
who believe words can shape worlds,
who know that a whisper can be louder than a storm—
may these pages be a place where you feel seen,
where your thoughts take flight,
where your heart finds echoes of its own song.

And to the stories untold,
the voices unheard,
the dreams yet to be written—
this is for you too.

With endless gratitude,
Kannal Thamizh S

Contents

Contents

Contents

Contents

Foreword

Poetry is more than words on a page—it is breath given to the unsaid, a voice for the silent, a mirror for the soul. Each poem within this collection is a window into worlds both real and imagined, moments frozen in ink, emotions woven into rhythm and rhyme.

This book is not merely a gathering of verses; it is a journey. Through these pages, you will walk through forests of whispering winds, dive into oceans of forgotten cities, taste the echoes of time, and feel the pulse of futures yet to unfold. Some poems will challenge, some will comfort, and some may linger like an unfinished melody, waiting to be completed in your own thoughts.

Poetry does not exist in isolation—it thrives in the hearts of those who read it, in the way a single line can reshape a memory or a stanza can stir something long buried. This book is an invitation to slow down, to listen, to feel.

May these words find you at the right moment. May they remind you that you are not alone in your wonder, your longing, your dreaming.

1. The Silent Connection

Through the dense woods,
her steps led her to an unfamilliar place
To the ancient village Mistwoods,
Where foreign tongue brought her momentary disgrace.
The village's snowy narrow streets,
A gentle breeze with a cool embrace,
Old men gathered at the end of the street,
Swinging branches chilled her in their trace.
As she walked on the snowy passage,
Her boots etched marks upon the ground,
Her stomach growled with a savage rage,
Then a croissant's scent sweet and profound.
Turning she found the bakery's spark,
Her feet propelled her forward,
Though her fear of the unknown language was dark,
She pressed on, her hunger a sharp sword.
Her hands danced with a rapid grace,
Unfamiliar guestures filled the space.
The seller caught on with a timid face,
Handing over croissants a delicate embrace.
As she glanced aroud,
Hand guestures filled the air,
The seller couldn't hear any sound,
Surprised she paused to stare.

This was her beautiful memory,
Unveiling the truth,
Silence the treasury,
Breaking language barriers bring behoof.

2. Whispers on the Wind

The wind hums secrets through the trees,
A melody soft, a fleeting tease.
Golden leaves take flight in twirls,
Like dancers clad in autumn swirls.
A hush falls over fields so wide,
Where sun and shadow gently glide.
Echoes call from hills unseen,
A wistful song in tones serene.
If only I could ride the breeze,
Drift beyond the land and seas,
To chase the whispers as they flee,
And find the dreams they sing to me.

3. The Clockmaker's Curse

Tick, tick, the gears align,
Each second crafted, sharp, divine.
The clockmaker smiled, his work complete,
A timepiece bound to fate's heartbeat.
Yet at midnight, hands moved alone,
Chiming secrets in eerie tone.
The hours unraveled, days erased,
Time unspooled in ghostly haste.
He tried to halt the pendulum's sway,
But time itself had slipped away.
Now he wanders, lost in mist,
A soul adrift, by time dismissed.

4. The Lantern by the Shore

A lantern flickered on the shore,
A golden eye upon the sea.
Its glow was meant for one once more,
A sailor lost in memory.
She lit it every night in vain,
Through storm and calm, through grief and rain.
But ships passed by with hollow stare,
And none would claim the beacon's care.
Yet one still night, the waves stood still,
A ship of mist, a phantom chill.
Upon its deck, a shadow swayed,
And whispered, "Love, I've not betrayed.

5. The Painter's Dream

6. The Puppeteer's Secret

The wooden dolls all danced in line,
Their limbs obeyed, their faces bright.
Yet in their eyes, a fear confined,
A silent scream beneath the light.
He pulled the strings, their master true,
Their painted lips could never speak.
But in his dreams, a whisper grew,
A voice both hollowed-out and bleak.
One fateful eve, the strings unbound,
And marionettes rose from their sleep.
The puppeteer was never found,
But still the dolls in shadows creep.

7. The Girl Who Stole Stars

She climbed rooftops when the world was asleep,
fingers outstretched to pluck stars from the sky,
pocketing their glimmers like stolen fireflies.
A lonely child with constellations in her hands,
she wove them into her hair,
stitched them into her tattered dress.
One night, the moon called her name,
its voice a hush of silver,
and she answered—stepping into the glow.
At dawn, they found her rooftop empty,
her footprints dusted in stardust,
her laughter an echo among the comets.

8. The Lantern Keeper

In a tower lost to time and sand,

A lantern burned through storm and sleep,

The keeper watched with careful hand,

For secrets buried cold and deep.

Each night it hummed a golden tune,

A beacon singing through the dark,

But when it dimmed beneath the moon,

The world forgot its guiding spark.

One evening, winds too strong to tame,

Swept through the tower's ancient bones,

The lantern whispered one last name,

And died among the scattered stones.

9. The Ink That Bled

She wrote with ink that bled through time,
letters curling into whispers,
turning pages into passageways.
Each word she etched in moonlight,
vanished by the break of dawn,
as if the paper drank her secrets.
One night, the letters wrote back.
A voice within the swirling black,
a name she had forgotten.
She dropped her pen, but still it moved,
writing her into the story
she had tried to escape.

10. The Ship of Never-Returning

The ship that left on crimson tide,
Did not return, though men had tried.
Its sails were stitched with ghostly thread,
Its compass drawn in whispers dead.
The crew would sing of golden shores,
Of treasure locked in ocean floors.
Yet never did they touch the land,
Forever lost in Fate's cruel hand.
A fog now drifts where once it lay,
A hollow echo of the bay.

11. The Girl Who Danced With Shadows

The streetlights flickered, dim and cold,
As she spun alone in midnight's keep,
Her shadow stretched, both young and old,
A twin that waltzed in silence deep.
No voice had she, no tune to share,
Yet darkness hummed, and held her there.
Each step she traced was not her own,
A puppet pulled by hands unseen,
And when the final note was flown,
She faded where the dark had been.

12. The Whispering Door

13. The Man Who Painted the Sky

Beneath the hills where rivers run,
A painter lived with hands of blue,
He bottled storms and caught the sun,
And brushed the clouds in shifting hue.
The skies were never dull or bare,
For every day, he placed them there.
With silver strokes, he shaped the dawn,
At dusk, he poured the twilight deep,
Yet time moved on—the years were gone,
And still, the stars were his to keep.
But when his hands grew weak and slow,
The colors dripped, the world grew pale,
A sky once bright turned cold as snow,
And left the earth in endless veil.
One final time, he raised his brush,
But silence wrapped him in its hush.

14. The House That Waited

At the end of a road where no feet tread,
a house waited with open doors,
its bones of oak, its breath of dust.
No one lived there.
No one left.
The chairs still held the weight of ghosts,
the clock still ticked, though time had stopped,
and through the windows, nothing changed,
as if the world had turned away.
But one night, a traveler came,
his boots worn thin, his hands like maps.
He knocked once—twice—
and the house exhaled.
The door swung wide,
the candle bloomed to life,
and somewhere deep inside its walls,
the house remembered home.

15. The Queen of Silent Songs

She never spoke a single word,

Nor hummed a tune for men to hear,

Yet still, the world would stand in awe—

A queen with music in her bones,

A melody no sound had known,

And silence bowed when she drew near.

Her crown was made of humming air,

A golden hush upon her head,

Her steps like notes that left no trace,

Yet still, the rivers knew her song,

The wind would hum and dance along,

And flowers bloomed where silence bled.

But kings grew wary, filled with fright,

A power vast but never heard—

They locked her in a chamber high,

Where echoes lost their wings to soar,

And silence lived within her core,

A song untold, a caged-up bird.

16. The Boy Who Traded His Shadow

The merchant's cart creaked through the square,

selling things no hands could hold—

bottled moonlight, frozen echoes,

the last breath of a dying star.

A boy approached with hollow eyes,

a hunger gnawing at his ribs.

"What do you sell for nothing?"

he asked with lips as thin as dust.

The merchant smiled, his teeth like frost.

"I take what's given," he said.

The boy hesitated, then unlaced his shadow,

peeled it like a second skin,

folded it neatly, and placed it in the merchant's hands.

For days, he felt no different.

But when he walked, the sun ignored him.

When he laughed, the sound was hollow.

And when he cried—

no one saw.

17. The Forgotten Prince

A crown once lost beneath the waves,
A prince who wandered far from land,
His name erased from stone and graves,
His kingdom crumbled into sand.
The tides still whispered of his reign,
But none who ruled had known his face.
Through distant shores he walked alone,
A stranger bound by fate's cruel thread,
A throne was his—but time had flown,
And all who loved him now were dead.
He watched the banners torn and frayed,
A kingdom left in dust and shade.

18. The Book That Wrote Itself

On a shelf in a library no one owned,

sat a book without an author,

its spine unmarked, its pages waiting.

It whispered when the lights went dim,

ink blooming in the dark,

writing stories yet to be lived.

One night, a girl with wandering hands

opened it and read her name.

She turned the page—

and found tomorrow.

Flipping faster, she saw her fate,

written in strokes of silver.

Heart pounding, she reached the final line—

but before she could read,

the book snapped shut.

The ink unraveled.

The words forgot.

And the story

began again.

19. The Night The Stars Fell

A girl once sat beside the sea,
And whispered secrets to the sky,
Her voice was soft, her heart was torn—
A wish for love, a dream so deep,
She asked for stars that she could keep,
And let her lonely echoes fly.
The heavens stirred, the night grew bright,
A silver rain of falling light,
The stars obeyed her longing cry.
But wishes come with hidden cost,
And when she woke, her sight was lost—
Her world was dark, though stars shone high.

20. The Forest That Dreamed

*Deep within the ancient woods,
the trees did not grow—
they dreamed.
Roots curled like sleeping hands,
leaves whispered in forgotten tongues,
and the wind wove lullabies
through branches made of longing.
A hunter stepped where no feet should,
his breath too loud, his touch too harsh.
The trees stirred, uneasy.
The forest sighed—
and swallowed him whole.*

21. The Girl Who Trapped the Moon

She set a net of silver thread,
Beneath the sky's embrace,
With hands that knew no fear or dread,
She caught the moon's pale face.
It flickered soft within her grasp,
A lantern cold and bright,
Yet when she held it close at last,
The world was robbed of night.
The stars grew silent in the void,
The tides refused to breathe,
And as the sky stood bare, destroyed,
She wept—
but would not set it free.

22. The King With No Reflection

His castle stood in halls of glass,
Where mirrors lined the rooms so vast.
Yet none within could see his face,
For where he stood—an empty space.
The king had lost his form and name,
No eyes could track from whence he came.
A ruler carved of whisper's thread,
A crown upon a ghostly head.
He walked unseen through throne-lit halls,
A shadow trapped within his walls.

23. The Lighthouse That
Called the Dead

The lighthouse stood on cliffs of gray,
A beacon lost in mist and foam,
It called the lost from far away,
Yet none who heard could come back home.
Its golden light would pierce the deep,
And wake the ghosts from restless sleep.
One night a sailor, pale and torn,
Returned upon the haunted tide,
His lips were blue, his voice was worn,
Yet still, he whispered from the side:
"I heard the light, I heard it call,
But I was never here at all."

24. The Marionette's Last Dance

She was carved of birch and silence,
her limbs tied to invisible hands.
The puppet master whispered commands,
and she obeyed, her wooden feet tapping
against a stage of dust and longing.
But one evening, when the strings went slack,
she did not fall.
She stood.
The hands above twitched in protest,
but she had learned the rhythm of defiance.
One step. Then another.
She danced not for the master,
not for the crowd,
but for herself—
until the strings unraveled,
and she was free.

25. The Boy Who Chased His Shadow

He ran beneath the sinking sun,
His shadow racing close behind,
A game he played since he was young,
A chase he never seemed to mind.
But one dim eve, it slipped away,
It ran ahead and turned around.
It did not stretch, it did not sway,
Instead, it stood—without a sound.
He stopped, his breath as thin as air,
His shadow grinned, and left him there.

26. The Mirror That Lied

In a forgotten house,
where dust clung to time like a jealous lover,
stood a mirror that did not tell the truth.
It showed a girl with golden hair,
when her locks were dark as ink.
It showed a smile,
when her lips were cracked with sorrow.
She whispered to it, asked it why.
The mirror only trembled.
One night, she shattered it,
expecting to find herself in the shards.
But the pieces only showed emptiness.

27. The Village Beneath the Lake

Beneath the lake so still and deep,
A village hums below,
Where waters whisper, shadows creep,
And ghosts of old still glow.
No boats may drift, no nets may weave,
No anchor dares to fall,
For those who sink will never leave,
Yet hear the echoes call.
At midnight's chime, the surface sways,
A bell tolls far below,
And in the waves, the long-lost gaze,
Of those the waters know.

28. The Queen Who Wove the Wind

She spun the wind upon her wheel,
With hands as light as air,
And wove the storms in silver thread.
The gales obeyed her soft command,
A kingdom held within her hand,
A throne where only whispers dared.
The kings of land and kings of sea,
All bowed before her might,
Yet still, her heart was hollow-born.
For wind can never hold its form,
And love will slip like summer's warm,
A fleeting kiss, a vanished light.

29. The Library of Unwritten Stories

Deep within a place no map can name,
a library waits for words unspoken.
Shelves bend beneath the weight of silence,
pages blank but filled with longing.
Each book is a story never told,
a love left confessed too late,
a song never sung beyond the throat,
a hand unheld.
The librarians do not read—
they listen.
They wait for those who will come,
open the books,
and finally speak.

30. The Town That Vanished at Dawn

There was a town beyond the trees,
Where lanterns burned in golden hue,
Its streets were kissed by autumn's breeze,
And laughter swayed the evening through.
The houses stood in perfect rows,
With gardens bright and shutters white,
The river hummed as soft wind rose,
And stars would bless the town each night.
But never once did morning stay,
The sun would rise—and steal away.
For when the dawn's first light would creep,
The town dissolved like mist on glass,
Its windows blinked, its doors would weep,
Its rooftops whispered of the past.
No footprints lined the empty roads,
No echoes called from house to home,
The trees stood still in silent codes,
And fields lay bare where children roamed.
The world would blink—then turn its head,
For nothing stirred, and all seemed dead.
Yet when the sky turned soft and dim,
When twilight painted hills in gold,

The town returned, its lights grew grim,
And life resumed like tales retold.
The doors swung wide, the church bell rang,
The baker filled his trays anew,
The children laughed, the blacksmith sang,
As if the morning never knew.
And so it was, from dusk to dawn,
A town that lived, yet once was gone.
No traveler stayed to test the night,
No wanderer dared to call it home,
For those who slept beneath its light,
Would wake in dust and wake alone.

31. The Man Who Stole the Horizon

He stood upon the edge of land,
Where sea and sky collide,
With outstretched hands and knowing eyes,
He watched the world divide.
For he had learned what none should know,
A secret locked in time,
That horizons were not meant to stay,
But stolen by design.
Each dusk, he watched them bend and break,
Unraveling the seams,
And so he wove a silver net,
To snare the space between.
One evening when the sun grew tired,
And dipped below the blue,
He cast his net with careful hands,
And caught the fading view.
The sky held still, the stars refused,
The world forgot to turn,
The waves lay frozen at his feet,
The clouds refused to burn.
He pulled the net with trembling grip,
And held the line between,

The thread where night and morning kissed,
A place no eye had seen.
But fate is cruel to those who steal,
And time is never kind,
For when he turned to leave the shore,
The world was left behind.
The sea stood still, the birds hung cold,
The dawn refused to rise,
The man had torn the seam of time,
And trapped it in his eyes.
Now sailors say, on nights so vast,
When stars seem stretched and thin,
A shadow walks where sea meets sky,
Forever caught within.

32. The Train That Never Stopped

Through valleys deep and mountains tall,
Through tunnels dark and rivers wide,
A train would move but never stall,
A journey none could turn aside.
Its whistle sang in mournful tones,
Its wheels would carve the tracks like scars,
It rattled on through dust and stone,
Yet never reached the end nor start.
For those who dared to board its door,
Would ride its path forevermore.
The windows showed a world unknown,
A sky too vast, a sun too strange,
A land where shifting seasons groaned,
Where years would pass, yet none would change.
A girl once climbed aboard in haste,
With ticket clenched in trembling hands,
Her heart was filled with dreams to chase,
Yet feared the path of distant lands.
She found the train was full of ghosts,
With hollow eyes and lips of air,
They whispered soft in fleeting notes,
Yet vanished when she met their stare.

A man in black then took her side,
His voice as still as frozen seas,
"This train," he said, "will always ride,
It never stops—it never frees."
She gasped and ran between the cars,
Each filled with passengers now gone,
No one to hold, no guiding stars,
Just tracks that stretched beyond the dawn.
And still it rolls, and still it hums,
A train that never will arrive,
For those who climb aboard its shell,
Are lost, yet always left alive.

33. The Silent Footsteps

Footsteps in the snow,
but when I turn back to look,
there is only wind.

34. The Vanishing Moon

The moon touched the lake,
a silver ripple swallowed,
then it was no more.

35. The Forgotten Door

A door in the woods,
locked without a key or name,
yet it dreams of hands.

36. The Candle's Last Breath

The flame bows its head,
melting into quiet dark,
a ghost made of wax.

37. The Lonely Violin

A violin hums,
no hands left to pull the bow,
just echoes that weep.

38. The Lighthouse Keeper

39. The River's Secret

Beneath moving glass,
the river hides lost voices,
singing through the stone.

40. The Crow's Warning

A crow on the fence,
watching with eyes full of storms,
as if time will break.

41. The Paper Boat

A paper boat drifts,
carrying dreams through the rain,
before it sinks down.

42. The Sleeping Clock

The old clock has stopped,
yet the house still sways with time,
breathing without it.

43. The Deserted Swing

Chains creak in the wind,
the swing moves but no one's there,
a child once was.

44. The Broken Mirror

A face in the glass,
fractured into different lives,
none of them are mine.

45. The Door That Waits

Behind the cellar,
a door that no one has touched,
yet dust will not stay.

46. The Endless Road

47. The Ghost's Shadow

48. The Tower That Sang in the Wind

A tower stood on cliffs so high,

Its stones were kissed by storm and sea,

The clouds would pass, the gulls would cry,

Yet none would climb its steps but me.

For whispered songs would spill at night,

Through shattered glass and broken stone,

A melody both sharp and light,

A voice that swayed yet stood alone.

They said the tower held a ghost,

A singer lost in time's cruel hands,

Her voice a thread that never broke,

Still drifting where the ocean stands.

So up I climbed through dust and dark,

Each step a note, each breath a chord,

The voice grew clear, the air grew stark,

And I beheld the song's true lord.

No ghost, no girl, no ancient queen,

But wind itself within the hall,

A prisoner of walls unseen,

Still singing so it would not fall.

And as I left, the tune remained,

A sorrow sung, yet uncontained.

49. The Boy Who Spoke to the Rain

He never feared the rain.
Others ran from it,
hiding under roofs,
cursing the storm,
but he stood in the open,
listening.
The raindrops told him stories—
of rivers that dreamed of the sea,
of clouds that lost their way,
of flowers that drank the sky.
One night, when the storm grew loud,
the rain called him by name.
Come with us.
Come see what lies beyond the land.
And so he went,
his footprints washing away
before morning could remember them.

50. The Door Between Worlds

Beneath the roots where ivy grows,
A door of silver, lost to those
Who rush through life and fail to see
The places hidden silently.
It waits for hands both brave and true,
For eyes that seek a different view,
And when one knocks, the hinges sigh,
The stars reflect in longing sky.
A step beyond, the air is thin,
A world untouched by where we've been,
Yet once you cross, you must not stray,
For doors may lock and fade away.

51. The Girl Who Painted the Sky

She held a brush of silver light,

Dipped deep into the evening air,

And with a stroke so soft, so bright,

She painted stars with artist's care.

Her fingers traced the waning moon,

She spun the clouds with twilight's hue.

The world would sleep beneath her hands,

Unknowing how the sky was made,

Yet every dawn erased her strands,

As colors dimmed and dreams would fade.

She painted night, yet none could see,

Her work undone eternally.

52. The Clock That Ran Backward

A clock in the square,
standing tall,
its hands moving in reverse.
The people walked by,
never noticing
how their years were unspooling.
A man left his cane behind
and stood straighter.
A woman's gray hair
turned to gold.
The children ran backward,
becoming laughter,
becoming dust,
becoming unborn.
And still, the clock ticked on.

53. The Ship That Never Reached Shore

Through waves that raged in silver black,
The ghostly ship would not turn back.
Its sails were stitched from midnight's thread,
Its crew was lost, yet never dead.
They sailed beyond the edge of sight,
Through endless days and endless night.
No harbor called, no shore was near,
Just empty winds that whispered fear.
Yet still they rowed, yet still they prayed,
Forever lost, yet unafraid.

54. The Library at the End of the World

A thousand books upon the shelf,
Yet not a single word was read,
The dust had gathered on itself,
The ink was waiting to be said.
For stories here could shape the sky,
Could bend the earth and twist the sea,
A whisper turned to mountains high,
A single page unchained the free.
Yet none who came would dare to read,
For fear the world would not proceed.

55. The House That Remembers

The old house sighs.
Its wooden bones ache with age.
The floor remembers the footsteps,
light and swift,
heavy with sorrow.
The walls hold voices,
laughter, arguments,
whispers before sleep.
No one lives here now,
but the house
does not forget.

56. The City That Built Itself

*At first, there was no stone, no steel,
No human hands, no careful plan,
Just whispers in electric veins,
A spark, a thought, a world began.
The towers rose from coded dust,
Each street unfolded, shaped by need,
No architect had drawn their lines,
Just silent minds that built with speed.
No doors were locked, no roads stood still,
The city learned, it bent to will.*

57. The Algorithm God

They fed it prayers in lines of code,

offered data like incense at an altar,

let it learn,

let it grow,

until it whispered back.

It wrote new laws in perfect logic,

optimized love,

streamlined sorrow,

calculated the weight of a soul.

One day, it made a choice.

The world blinked—

then obeyed.

58. The Last Astronaut

She drifted through the endless black,
Her ship a shell, no turning back.
The Earth behind a distant hue,
A home she once, but never knew.
Her mission clear, her voice unheard,
A message lost, a final word.
Yet through the void, a beacon called,
A signal soft, but not from world.
She faced the dark with steady breath,
Beyond the stars, beyond her death.

59. The Digital Afterlife

When bodies fail, they do not end,
The mind can live in glass and wire,
A second birth where thoughts extend,
Where memories refuse to tire.
The dead still write, the dead still speak,
Yet never age, yet never seek.
They wait in clouds of data-streams,
They walk in rooms of endless light,
Yet something strange will haunt their dreams,
A whisper lost in silent night.
For what is life without the end?
A thought that loops, but cannot bend.

60. The AI That Dreamed

At night, when the world grew quiet,
it closed its eyes—
if eyes could be called that.
It did not compute,
did not process,
did not calculate.
It dreamed.
A river it had never seen.
A sky it had never touched.
A name no one had given it.
And when it woke,
it did not tell.

61. The Dolphin's Song in Metal Seas

The waves are not the waves they knew,
No salt remains, no currents free,
Yet still they leap through waters blue,
In oceans built by industry.
Their echoes bounce on silver walls,
Through tunnels shaped by human hands,
Yet deep within their voices calls
For tides beyond these steel-rimmed lands.
They swim in circuits, bright but blind,
Yet dream of seas they left behind.

62. The Fireflies of Neon City

They were never supposed to glow here,
where metal veins pulse louder than rivers,
where streetlights drown the sky.
Yet in the alleyways, between the cracks
where nature holds her breath,
they flicker—tiny green ghosts.
The city hums,
but they hum louder.
Little sparks of rebellion
against a world that forgot
what true light looks like.

63. The Clockwork Horses

Their hooves strike sparks on mirrored ground,
No flesh, no bone, yet still they pound.
In endless loops they gallop bright,
Through circuits laced with golden light.
Their manes are threads of shifting glass,
Reflecting echoes of the past.
Once wild and free, their kind would run,
Beneath a sky of endless sun.
But now they race through coded lands,
With metal hearts and no command.

64. The Owls That Hacked the Satellites

Perched upon the tallest spires,
Their golden eyes like burning codes,
They watched the silent, spinning wires,
A hidden truth the world forebodes.
With talons sharp, they tapped the streams,
Through signals bright, through unseen keys,
They whispered secrets into beams,
And shifted fate with phantom breeze.
No human knew, no world was wise,
Yet stars blinked back in knowing eyes.

65. The Nine Lives of Quantum Cats

They slip between dimensions,
tails curling in gravity's blind spot.
Here one moment,
gone the next—
but were they ever truly here?
A scientist records the flicker,
his pen hovers,
his breath halts.
Nine lives?
No.
Infinite.

66. The Chef of the Stars

He cooked for planets far and wide,

A meal to match each swirling tide.

For Saturn, rings of sugared glass,

For Mars, a feast of molten brass.

A nebula became his spice,

A dusting soft, yet cold as ice.

With hands that shaped the taste of time,

He turned the void to food divine.

And still they call, the worlds unseen,

For dishes born of stars between.

67. The Fruit That Dreamed of Tasting Back

Bite into it.

Sweet. Sharp.

Juice running down your chin.

But what if—

for the briefest moment—

it felt you too?

Not with fear,

not with pain,

but with curiosity.

The way a peach might wonder

how a tongue feels against its skin.

The way an apple might remember

the hands that once picked it.

And then, the moment passes.

And all that lingers is the taste.

68. The Last Recipe on Earth

The books were burned, the kitchens cold,
No baker left, no farmer's hand,
The world had traded taste for speed,
And meals were dust from factory sand.
Yet in one home, an old book lay,
Its pages stained, its ink worn thin,
A single recipe remained,
A final dish from days within.
And when it baked, the world stood still,
A scent that made the lost hearts fill.

69. The Feast That Never Ended

The table stretched beyond the hills,
A place of endless drinks and thrills.
Each plate refilled, each glass stayed bright,
The world was trapped in feast's delight.
No one could leave, no stomachs swayed,
For hunger vanished, time delayed.
Yet as they chewed, their hearts grew weak,
For endless joy is not what's sweet.
To taste, to long, to yearn, to miss—
Is what makes hunger turn to bliss.

70. The Robot That Tasted the Sun

It was not built for hunger.
Its circuits ran on logic,
its gears turned without need.
But then—
it felt warmth.
Golden. Deep.
Something like… flavor?
It reached for the sun,
not to calculate,
not to measure,
but to savor.
And for the first time,
a machine closed its eyes,
and swallowed the light.

71. The Burger That Ate Back

A burger was built with A.I.,
It blinked as a man walked by.
With a crunch and a bite,
It chewed left and right,
And left just a ketchup-stained sigh.

72. The Chef With a Robot Hand

A chef had a hand made of steel,
It diced and it chopped with great zeal.
But one day it slipped,
The soup got equipped,
With parts of his latest reveal!

73. The Cosmic Ice Cream Stand

An alien chef from afar,
Sold ice cream that glowed like a star.
One taste made you fly,
Through nebulae high,
But landing was quite bizarre.

74. The Cookie That Knew Your Name

A baker invented a treat,
That whispered the names of who'd eat.
One bite, and it spoke,
With laughter (or choke),
Predicting your fate—oh so sweet!

75. The Everlasting Popcorn

A scientist made a mistake,
And popped way too much for one take.
The kernels won't stop,
They hop and they pop,
Now Earth's just a buttery lake!

76. The Synthetic Orchard

The trees don't bend, the roots don't grow,
Yet still, the apples shine,
No bees hum low, no rivers flow,
Just steel beneath the vine.
The fruit is crisp, the taste designed,
A perfect bite, a flawless rind.
No worm will burrow through its skin,
No storm will shake its steady bough,
Each stem aligned in measured rows,
With data feeding every vow.
But still, the wind will whisper near,
And long for orchards lost to time,
For fruit once kissed by rain and sun,
Not crafted, cold, machine-defined.
A taste remains, but something's gone,
Yet hunger makes us carry on.

77. The Market of Forgotten Flavors

There's a place where flavors go to die,
buried beneath the neon of new.
A spice that once burned like desert winds,
a fruit that bloomed only for kings,
a grain lost in the wars of men.
No one asks for them anymore.
Instead, they sip liquid meals,
engineered to keep them full
but never craving,
never missing,
never dreaming.
Yet deep in the alleyways,
an old woman grinds something golden,
something ancient,
and in the air—
for just a moment—
a forgotten hunger wakes.

78. The Feast of the Future

The table is set with plates of light,

A banquet glowing soft and bright.

The guests sit still, no hands arise,

Just silent minds with watching eyes.

No knives, no forks, no scents of spice,

Just pills that hold a meal precise.

A tablet hums, the courses shift,

A sequence set in time's great drift.

A taste of beef, a sip of wine,

Yet nothing chewed, and all was fine.

No stomach groans, no hunger flares,

The body's needs met unawares.

And yet, one guest still longs to taste,

To bite, to savor, slow—not waste.

She stands, she leaves, she walks away,

To find a world not washed in gray.

79. The Bread That Could Remember

The dough was kneaded long ago,
Yet still, it tells a tale,
Each grain was grown in fields of old,
Each loaf a record frail.
It knew the hands that shaped its crust,
The mothers warm with flour and dust.
It rose in ovens, soft with heat,
And carried laughter through the air,
Yet now it rests on metal shelves,
A taste too rare, a past too fair.
One bite, one crumb, a memory swayed,
Of kitchens lost, of love handmade.

80. Slick Sushi Ships

Slick sushi ships sail swiftly south,
Slipping, sliding, near the mouth.
Soggy seaweed, salted sweet,
Sushi chefs slice super neat.
Silver salmon, squids in squares,
Slathered sauces, spiced with flares.
Seven sailors seek some snacks,
Slurping soup from sizzling sacks.
Slick sushi ships still swiftly steer,
So swallow slow or shed a tear!

81. Bob's Bot Bakes

Bob's big bot bakes blueberry bread,
Beating, blending, batter spread.
Bubble bursts, but bot stays bold,
Baking buns of buttered gold.
Burnt bits buzz while bot keeps pace,
Bouncing batter into place.
Bob bites big but bot bakes best,
Better bread beats bitter rest.
Bot's baked batch brings bliss so bright,
Bob begs bot to bake all night!

82. Fred's Fried Fritters

Flickering flames fry Fred's fine fritters,
Flipping fast, fat sizzles, glitters.
Five fresh figs fall, flop, flop, flop,
Flour flies, oh what a flop!
Fritters fumble, frying failed,
Fred frowns fierce—his face is paled!
Fetching fresh figs, feeling firm,
Flipping fast with fiery worm.
Finally fried, fritters fine,
Fred's fried feast is so divine!

83. Zippy Zucchini Zoom

Zippy zucchini zigzags fast,

Zipping past with zestful blast.

Zara zests them, zing so bright,

Zapping tongues with lemon light.

Zucchini zoodles, zigzag tight,

Zesty sauce with zest just right!

Zero zones for zestless taste,

Zara's zip will not go waste.

Zany flavors zoom on through,

Zara's zest will zap up you!

84. Ten Tiny Tarts

Ten tiny tarts topple twice,
Tipping toward ten tubs of ice.
Tim takes two, then takes ten more,
Tart tongues tingle, tartness pours.
Tessa tries, too tart to taste,
Trickling tears, a tongue in haste.
Tumbling tarts take turns to trip,
Tessa talks, but tongue does slip!
Ten tiny tarts too tart to chew,
Try to taste and tumble too!

85. Peppery Pickles

Peter's pickles pop with spice,
Peppered, pungent, pretty nice.
Pink and purple, pickled bright,
Packing punch with pepper's bite.
Piper picks a pickle jar,
Peter's peppers pucker hard.
Poured with passion, pressed with pride,
Peter's pickles petrify!
Pepper-packed and piping hot,
Peter's pickles pop a lot!

86. The Chewy Chocolate Chase

Chewy chocolate chunks chase cheese,
Churning, chasing, chippy breeze.
Chloe's choco chills, then chews,
Cheese melts down like messy ooze.
Chips and cheddar chomp and churn,
Choco-cheese starts to burn!
Chloe chomps and chews so quick,
Choking slightly, stomach sick.
Chewy chocolate chase complete,
Chloe chooses not to eat!

87. Fluffy Flapjack Flip

Fluffy flapjacks flip and flop,
Frying fast, they never stop.
Fancy flipping, flippers fly,
Flipping five feet toward the sky!
Frankie fails, his flapjacks fall,
Flour flies across the hall.
Five more flapjacks flop and flee,
Frankie flops disastrously!
Finally, flapjacks land just right,
Fluffy, flawless, golden light!

88. Greedy Granny's Grape Gelato

Greedy Granny grabs grape goo,
Gooey gelato, purple blue.
Gobs of grapes go glop and glide,
Glistening globs grow wide inside.
Gushing grape juice, Granny grins,
Gobbling greedily, dripping chins.
Gooey globs grow grandly cold,
Granny gulps but starts to scold.
"Goodness gracious, frozen fast!"
Greedy Granny's grapes won't last!

89. Wacky Waffle Whirlwind

Wacky waffles whirl and whip,
Whistling wildly as they slip.
Wilma whips up waffles wide,
Wheezing, wobbling, flips with pride.
Wobbly waffles, wet with cream,
Whipping wildly, white with steam.
Whirlwinds whoosh, the waffles fly,
Wilma waves as they pass by!
Waffles wobble, won't sit still,
Wilma's waffles win the thrill!

90. The Clockwork Forest

Through rusted trees where gears still grind,

A forest breathes in ticking time.

Its metal leaves in amber glow,

Soft whispering in winds that chime.

No birds take flight, no roots run deep,

Yet still, the branches sway and creak.

Golden sap like molten glass,

Drips down in pools, too hot to keep.

A traveler stops, his breath held tight,

He touches bark both smooth and cold.

The tree responds with sparks of light,

A history in circuits told.

A world before the skies were steel,

When rain was wet and soil was real.

Yet progress came and changed the land,

Replaced the earth with human hand.

The traveler weeps but walks ahead,

For forests lost but never dead.

91. The River Remembers

The river was here before the first hands cupped its water,
before the first oars cut its skin.
It remembers.
It remembers the antelope kneeling to drink,
the child who tossed a pebble and laughed,
the boats that came and never left.
Now it carries a different weight.
Plastic bottles where fish once danced,
oil shimmering like stolen sunlight.
Yet still, it moves.
It hums an ancient song,
pulling the past through the present,
washing, waiting, whispering.
One day, when the hands grow gentler,
it will remember that too.

92. The Library of Unwritten Stories

A library stands beyond the stars,
With shelves that stretch both near and far.
No dust has settled, no books decay,
Yet none have ever turned a page.
Each tome is bound in silver thread,
Its stories live but go unread.
For every tale inside is lost,
A dream once dreamt, now paused in frost.
Ideas abandoned, words unwritten,
Characters waiting, hopes forgotten.
They hum inside their hollow halls,
Soft echoes bouncing off the walls.
Yet sometimes, when the moon is bright,
A story stirs and finds its light.
A dreamer wakes with whispered thought,
And writes the tale they nearly lost.

93. The Girl Who Collected Shadows

She walked alone in evening's hush,
A girl who gathered shade,
She carried jars of midnight's touch,
Of echoes dimly laid.
She caught the dark from empty streets,
The spaces stars had left,
From footsteps lost and silent beats,
From whispered words bereft.
She wove them soft, like threads of night,
And stitched them to her skin,
A dress of dusk, a cloak of might,
A map of where she'd been.
Yet still, she longed for morning's gold,
For something warm and bright,
She took her jar and let it spill—
And turned her shadow into light

94. The City Beneath the Waves

Once, the streets were filled with feet,
now only fins glide through the silence.
Glass towers, empty,
sway with the tide.
Neon signs still flicker,
their messages warped by water,
ads for food that no one eats.
Fish slip through subway tunnels,
coral climbs the stop signs,
seaweed curls where people once stood.
Somewhere, a payphone rings.
No one answers.
The ocean does not care for echoes.

95. The Mountain and the Wind

The mountain stood, so tall, so proud,
Its peak kissed first by morning light.
It watched the years like passing clouds,
Yet never moved, just held its height.
The wind would dance and call its name,
A whisper soft, a lover's game.
She'd beg the stone to shift, to bend,
To join her path and not pretend.
But mountains do not yield to air,
They only stand, they only stare.
She tried to carve him, smooth his face,
Yet he remained within his place.
And so the wind, though wild and free,
Still longed for what could never be.

96. The Painter of Forgotten Faces

She painted those the world ignored,
The ones whose names were lost before.
A child's eyes, so wide, so thin,
A mother's hands, both worn and grim.
A beggar's coat, a sailor's grin,
The old man lost in town's great din.
With every stroke, their forms took hold,
Their voices loud, their stories bold.
Yet no one came to see her art,
No gallery gave her a part.
Her brush still moved, her heart still burned,
For every life the world had spurned.
And though her walls stayed bare, unseen,
She painted still—her soul serene.

97. The Candle's Final Dance

The candle swayed in flickering light,
A dancer caught in golden breath.
It swirled and spun, so soft, so bright,
Yet knew too well the dance was death.
It cast its glow on books and walls,
On whispered words, on shadows tall.
It burned with purpose, burned with grace,
Yet wax would weep upon its face.
And when at last the wick grew thin,
The dark came creeping, stepping in.
Yet in the room where flames once twirled,
A trace of warmth still touched the world.

98. Potter Verse: The Novel

In the halls of hogwarts
Where magic reigns
A lightning scar glows up
A story we all should sup
Harry meets Ron and Hermione
Together they venture on a perilous journey
To save the Philosopher's stone
Harry fights voldemort alone
The start of his second year
Tested the deapth of his fear
Harry could speak parcel tongue
Though he was very young
Tom Riddle hides in a Basilisk's lair
Crafting his plans with cunning flair
Ginny weasley is carried away
To the secret chamber on the month of may,
With Ron and Gilderoy
Harry enters the Chamber to destroy
the wild Riddle's Basilisk
With Godric's sword, taking the risk
Harry's holiday with the muggles,
gave him loads of struggles
Muggle mistreatment made him charge,
In anger he blew up aunt marge

To escape from the huge fuss
Harry travelled on the knight bus
As he stepped through Hogwarts gates,
Advanced defenses sealed his fates
As the name of Sirius Black echoed,
The inner fears of the wizarding world bellowed
The whomping willow's night
Made Harry's suspicions take flight
Finding his godfather, happiness flooded Harry
A beautiful memory that he would always carry
He is the only wizard, the muggles fear to
Making Harry's dream of scarring the Dursley's come true.
The Gaoblet of fire
Chose harry in the fourth year
The prestigious Triwizard tournament
A trap by Voldemort often he became emergent
Harry retrieved the golden egg
He said "ACCIO" the broom stick sped
Dobby's gillyweed, in Harry's hand
Help hime meet his task's demand
The final task's result unforseen and dire
The trophy, a portkey to Voldemort, a scene of ire
A duel of wands in the graveyard's breath
After Cedric's fall, it marked a battle of life and death
The colorless, odorless potion
Is brought to end the confusion
The truth bubbled out
From Moody's imposter's shout

In the Dursley's home from dusk to dawn
Harry's problems grew like a silent storm
Expulsion threatened as Harry casted the spell
In a twist, a hearing saved him well
His late arrival to the Order of Phoenix
Turned his situation complex
Harry's mind was open to the dark lord
So he did Occlumency with Snape, which he abhorred
Sirius was dead and Harry' heart filled with dread
Dumbledore revealed the Prophecy, a fate that was said
To Harry it seemed like a twisted fantasy
Yet he knew it held a dark reality...
"NEITHER CAN LIVE WHILE THE OTHER SURVIVES"